Our Lost Pages

Haley Ballheim

BookLeaf Publishing

India | USA | UK

Presentation by *BookLeaf Publishing*

Web: www.bookleafpub.com

E-mail: info@bookleafpub.com

ISBN: 9789360945534

First edition 2024

To those who have experienced the complexities of love and loss, know this: within you resides a greatness and worthiness of love far beyond what you may perceive.

PREFACE

Writing serves as my emotional outlet, a means to grapple with the intensity of emotions and navigate the traumas that have marked my journey. "Our Lost Pages" encapsulates a series of poems born from those poignant moments and memories. This collection stands as a testament to the therapeutic power of expression, as the words within these pages have been my companions in confronting the challenges of life and heartbreak.

In sharing this book, I aspire for it to be a source of solace and resonance for others who may find kinship in the struggles and triumphs woven into the verses. "Our Lost Pages" is not just a collection; it is a cathartic journey through the labyrinth of emotions. As this marks the beginning, I envision it as the inaugural step in an ongoing exploration of the healing potential inherent in the art of writing. May these words extend a hand of understanding to those who traverse similar paths and inspire a sense of shared strength in the face of life's trials.

Lost Promises

When I write about us, I would like to write the chapters we never got to finish, the slow dances we never had, the late-night cooking, warm coffee mornings, weekend dates, and new beginnings in different cities. I'd love to write about your eyes, with the beauty they hold, it has the power to make my heart melt, they form smiles on my face with grace, and I'd never want to be lost anywhere else. I'd love to write about the slow mornings, the light spilling in from the window, the smell of coffee, eggs, and bacon. Us wrapped up, hearts beating, where in that moment no one exists but us, where the world slows, and time stops. I'd love to write about the kids we never had, a little girl, and a boy, the cutest most precious thing in the world, whom I would have given everything, and would do anything to watch grow up, to see the world through little eyes, before they are blinded by the world's darkness. I'd love to write about the ring you never gave me, the beautiful silk dress I never wore, the suit and tie you never did, the family that wasn't there, and all the moments we never had. I think I'm still left here daydreaming about the moon and stars, while you're somewhere in her arms.

Bittersweet

You showed me patience
You showed me love
You showed me care
You guided my hand through the darkness
You gave me things I never had
You made each moment extraordinary

I'm sorry
I'm sorry we were both broken
I'm sorry the pain overwhelmed us
I'm sorry we couldn't rescue ourselves

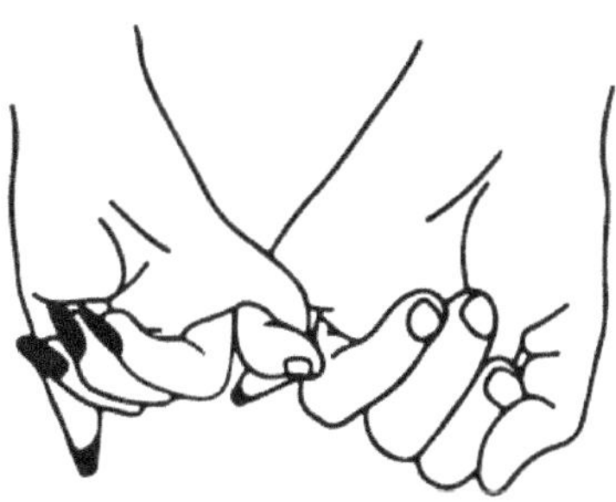

Plea

This is my plea
For you to return my heart to me
You left my chest cracked open
I'm pouring out the seems
Screaming in agony
Begging you to return it to me
Even if it's bruised or beaten
Even if there's nothing left
I need back the pieces that I gave
To repair this damage that you left

Seeing Silhouettes

I need to get out of this place because I still see silhouettes of your face

I smell your scent walking down the streets

I feel your voice breathing down my neck

I see your eyes in sunrises

I still feel your presence wrapped around my waist

It's like you never left

The wind carries echoes of your laughter

The roses cradle the memory of your smile

It makes me wanna stay for a while

But you held my heart in your hands

bled me dry and called it your trophy

Wine Glasses

I think the wine bottle keeps overfilling itself
It sits on the counter so that every time I miss
you
I can pour another glass
but it never empties
One glass
two glasses
three
four
then five
Still not empty
Like it knows the feeling of you never goes
away
It pours me another glass and imagine your
laugh
It pours another and I still see us dancing

It pours once more
And my heart just shatters
Dizzy and Delusional
Sobbing on the floor
Pathetically crying over someone who couldn't
give me more
I still see your face
As my rose-colored glasses break
And my heart aches
I loved you too much for my sake.

Looping Dreams

I'm writing this while you hold me in your arms, about love with roses and thorns. How for a second "I love you" didn't sound like a lie, and the taste of your lips made me feel like I could fly.

Then reality shatters the illusion

Writing this while you hold me in your arms, it was a dream mixed with reality. "I love you" becomes a deceptive echo, a trick played by my subconscious. Yet, reality insists that the declarations of love were genuine.

I wake up

Writing this while I lay on your chest, listening to the rhythm of your heartbeat, my heart finds refuge. In this space, love unfolds like the petals of spring flowers, delicate and hopeful, even in the face of the awakening dawn.

The Weight Of Despair

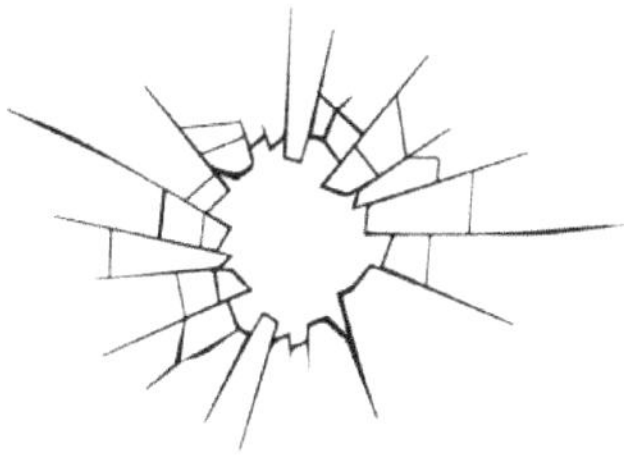

My eyes welded shut in the prison of my own tears.

My voice withered away.

My face turned blue, gasping for air without you.

A heart-wrenching explosion shattered my core.

Agony pulsating through every bone, my legs giving way to the weight of despair.

Desperate hands reaching for your face.

Only to find the cruel emptiness that mirrored my shattered soul.

A Heart's Silent Cry

I keep replaying our last night in my mind

The fight that almost happened

The weariness that hung heavy on us both

The memory vivid and tantalizing

laying on your arm, our fingers intertwined,
feeling your arms wrapped around me

Silent darkness enveloped us, the air between us
thickened, unspoken understanding in that
shared silence, our hearts craving and
surrendering to the magnetic pull of the moment

An undeniable hunger for more of you, an
insatiable desire that surpassed the mere
physicality of touch. In the hushed darkness, my
silent plea echoed, a plea for a connection that
went beyond skin, a thirst for an intimacy that
transcended the tangible.

Two Sides Of The Same Coin

Your love whispers through the gentle spring breeze, your heartbeat resonates in the melody of the sea, and the midnight sky becomes a masterpiece with the reflection of the depth of beauty in your eyes.

Suddenly, I feel like I'm falling.

Your love takes on a haunting allure, a spell that enchants and torments. The crashing waves carry the echoes of your whispered affections, The crashing waves carry echoes of your anguished screams, a torment that pierces through the silence. The fires you spark cast shadows that flicker like the haunting memories within the depths of your eyes.

My Heart Beats Only For You

You've abandoned me.

In a place where the air is thin.

My eyes sunken in despair.

My lips cracked, split, and bleeding.

My body is brittle, shattering with each breath.

My heart beats only for you.

And in this sea of torment, you've left me, a
ghost haunting the ruins of your absence.

Laying In A Bed Of Flowers

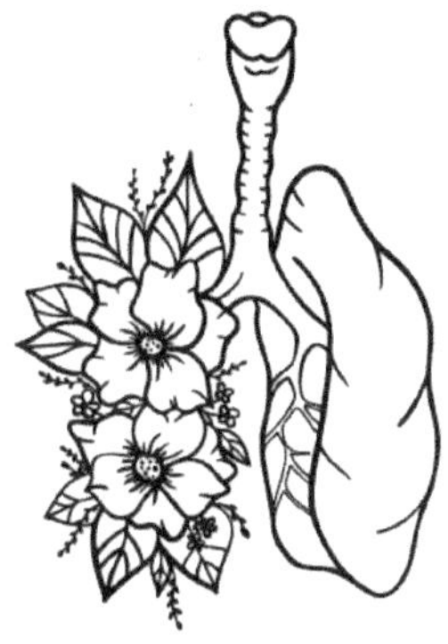

Lay me where I am loved.

Lock away my heart, assure me I am yours,
Promise me eternity.

Run through meadows with me, the flowers
mirroring my heart, and your eyes a beautiful
sight with the stars.

Love me more on days draped in gray, take it
slow, a bath to wash our sorrows away.

Morning sun, coffee cups in hand, kisses soft
and sweet.

In your gaze, I find a tranquil sea, here with you
is where I want to forever be.

Bouquet Of Death

There is a shelf filled with wilted blooms

stood as tokens of courteous deception

their petals once vibrant now dripping with
poison

Withered like your feelings for me

a tragic symbol to forever

crumbles with the shattered illusion of you and
me

Forever Yours

I desired you

though self-love eluded me

unmended my wounds

transitioning towards healing

climbing this hill of self-discovery

"You deserve more, you deserve better" they
spoke

I was warranted the universe

you were the universe

but you remained beyond my grasp

forevermore, forever yours.

Dry Wells And Stained Tears

You took it whenever you wanted

Even if my waterfalls ran dry

Even if my eyes said no

When my voice couldn't

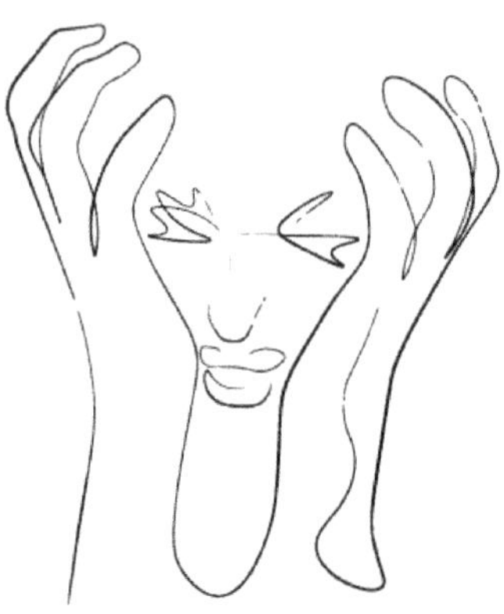

Living In Coffins

The dead and the living are one in the same

Because once people leave it doesn't matter if they still breathe

It'll feel all the same

"I'll Always love You"

You planted a kiss on my forehead, venom dripping from your words as you uttered, "I'll always love you." The last words you said as I pulled you from the drowning depths, and you pushed me in knowing I couldn't swim.

The Ferryman Takes His Price

I am a vessel full of pain.

I knew you were a bad idea and picked you anyway.

I felt all the warning signs echoing in the back of my mind, I saw all the pain in your eyes and wanted to take it away.

The sting of pain my hands felt hugging you, as I hugged you anyway, feeling myself slowly drift away.

I knew I needed to walk away, but no one picked me over everything. So I wanted to pick you, to love you, to show you what it felt like to have care, to be a thought in someone's mind all the time.

But it all came at a cost, I had to pay the price, and I hope at least in the end, in some universe that moment, that memory of all the good things about you and me, plays on repeat frozen in time.

Peeling Layers

Don't call me, because I won't answer the phone.
while that voice whispers in the back of my
mind, while I feel like I want to peel off my
skin, rip all the thoughts to shreds, gut out all my
feelings on the table. Should we bag it up? Put it
in the freezer, and save it for another time?
Another time I'm not so weak, but what has it
been? Days? Weeks? Months? Years? The
freezer is getting full, maybe I should just buy
another one to give me more time? But how
much time do I need? Will I ever be the same? I
stand at the freezer, peel another layer of skin,
place it inside, and you'd think it would be
enough. But I still feel your touch.

My Favorite Memory

You drove away, you couldn't even face me, you lacked the respect to even tell me goodbye. I ran up the stairs, a rush of memories flooded my mind. I didn't know if I expected to find you at the top or what I would say if you were, but your absence made my heart ache, feeling the weight of it all. I remembered our first night together, I remembered the night I made us dinner, with wine, the wine that caused flushed skin, that made us spill secrets, and steal touches in the dark. I remembered the first time you said you loved me, so quickly, so casually, between fits of laughter "god I love you" you said. I remembered the hands we held, the moments sat staring into your eyes thinking about how I wanted to tell you how beautiful you are. My favorite pastime was tracing the tattoos on your body. I remembered how you have dimples when you'd smile into our kiss, and I remember where we were when I first noticed it "You have dimples!" I shouted pulling away from our kiss, you just smiled at me in response, and I stared at your face with the biggest grin. As my mind raced through our shared history, each breath felt like shards of glass piercing my heart. It inevitably led me back to a night etched in my soul—the night I took you to my favorite spot beneath a star-lit sky, you looked up, while I looked at you, because you were my star, my everything. You were my favorite—your embrace, early morning moments bathed in soft sunlight, your kiss, your laughter, and the captivating shade of your eyes. Now, you exist solely as my favorite agonizing memory.

Idle mind

25

Our photographs sit behind my eyes
Our memories replay in my mind
I can still feel the touch of your skin
the taste of your lips
like you've only just left
But time moves differently here
Stuck in my mind
It's been months and I still can't shake you off
me
Sitting here like a corpse where you left me.

Bed With Chains

26

We spent a lot of time in your bed, like stepping into your room was something otherworldly, where moments of silence were bliss, conversations were shared, and laughter was made. The endless hours of sleeping next to each other meant everything to me. I could drift away in a memory of your sheets, tracing marks on your arms, and taking in your smell with my head on your chest. I love you meant something different to me, and you'll live here forever in my memory.

Crashing into the ground

I do not love softly.

I do not fall lightly.

I crash into you like a brick wall.

I plan our wedding three months into our relationship.

Call me insane.

Insane I shall be then.

If loving you makes me insane, lock me up, and throw away the key.

I'll tell the moon and stars about our love story instead.

And my heart will always be yours in the end.

You remind my inner child of her

I don't understand why you ask if I love you, I think you're crazy to ask such a thing. but then I remember the way I stare at your face with such blank expressions, though in my head I'm thinking of how lovely you are and, I'm hoping I see you tomorrow, and the next day, and the next day. I'm hoping that we get our happy ending and that you stay here forever with me.

Then your loud voice breaks through my train of thought "DO YOU EVEN LOVE ME?!"

The yelling feels like it rumbles through the whole house. I stare at you blankly, I am back in my family home, I'm 14, and I'm asking my mother why she doesn't love me, as she yells in my face, as she tells me I'm useless, as she shows me every way a mother isn't supposed to love you.

"I do love you" I say, and you tell me that I do not because I simply don't show it well enough, because my face is so blank when I say it, because I do not know how to love you like a normal person. And my silly bullying means I love you, and I hate you doesn't actually mean I hate you, it means I love you. Because I love you is too hard for me to say some days and I know it's not fair, that you don't deserve the way that I love. But call me selfish, 'cause I'm begging you to stay through it all; I'm trying I swear. Please don't give up on me, do not show me she was right when she said no one will love me.

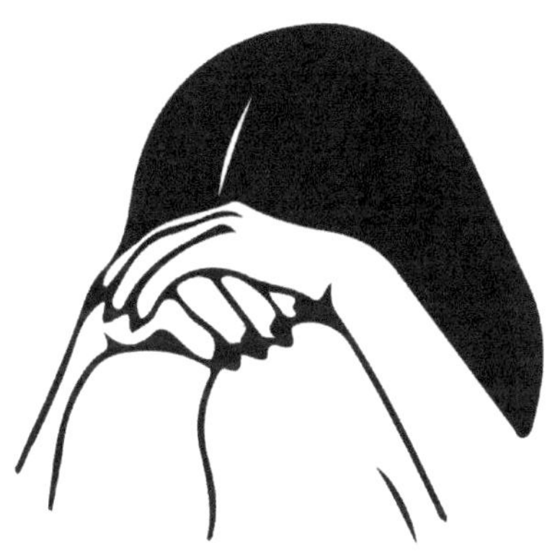

"like it was yesterday"

If my mind was a hall full of doors, there is a door there for you. A door that everyday I spend placing flowers on your grave. Then spend the afternoon with your ghost, and as evening dawns upon us, and the flowers start to wilt away. It tells me I'll have to come back tomorrow. For another day, another bouquet, another few hours I get to spend with what I have left of you. But there'll come a day that I'll have to let you go, but I can't, not today. So I'll lay some more flowers on your grave, and remember your smile like it was yesterday.

Pain is art

Who hurt you they ask me

well let me make you a list

it's just saying "Here take pity on me"

While I try to justify all the bad things I've done

There is no excuse

no excuses for all the hearts I've bruised

no excuses for the parts of you that I've left in
ruins

No excuse for this life I've chosen

So here I am making something beautiful

Beauty made of the ruins of all my pain

all the loss

all the bad days

Here, please find solace in this, please take all that I have and make art with it.

See this beauty in the pain, and celebrate life another day.

The ruins of war

I am Poison.

I am a pretty face, with a broken heart.

I am the calm, but also the storm.

I'll push you out the door, while all I wanted was for you to stay.

Stay but for what?

Why would you stay, stay just for me to get angry, to yell, to hold you to unreasonable standards?

Why stay, why would you stay for the pain that I bring, the bomb that I am.

The hurt that I hold over your head.

I am so convinced that you'll hurt me first, so I break us before you can.

I broke us, and as I stand in the ruins of us.

I am destroyed that I lost us.

Time Bomb

35

You pack all your things.

Just like I told you to.

You walk out the door.

And as I'm left here in this empty room.

I am clawing at the walls.

Sobbing in pain.

I can't get you back.

The memories of you and me

are still in this room.

I can't look away.

Their pain also brings me peace.

I was so scared of something breaking us.

That in the end, I was the bomb all along.

Warm Regards

"Your dad was always just happy to have kids," my oldest brother says to me on the phone, then he talks about our mother, and in the middle of it, I realize he got the unloving version of her like I did. I think they just hid it better, my siblings. I think they were still holding on to hope until the very end. How sad, a group of kids who just wanted to be loved, who had parents who acted as if they didn't want them at all. We're all grown up now, gone our own ways, and no longer speak. Unless of course you're calling for a birthday, if we don't forget. The toxic air that our parents breathed into our lungs when we were just children has followed us every step of the way. Failed relationships, bad marriages, mistreating our children, mental illnesses, not having friends, not having support systems, doing horrible things, pushing each other away, and each of us playing a part in destroying this family more than it already was. I somehow walked out of there alive, but the mental price I had to pay is still here, and this battle I've always had to fight alone.

signed,

Your "beloved" sister.

"You're Perfect"

You tell me I'm perfect while looking through wedding photographs. But I still see her in your eyes. It was the calm before the lies. You tell me I've hurt you, and that may be true but if I wasn't enough to make you stay in the first place, then maybe you didn't love me at all. Because you tell me I'm perfect, as if we're puzzle pieces that fit together, though your face doesn't show it, and your actions don't prove it. So please tell me where you're leaving all this so-called love, is it at her door? Is it kept in a safe in your heart for her? How about in a place I'll never have a key to, because I wasn't important enough for you, and maybe one day you'll realize I am good enough. but I'll be long gone before then. I won't stand around here being second place, second choice, the backup plan. No, it won't be me, I've got better places to be.

Drinking memories to stay alive

I think a part of me died when you left, I know
that's silly to say but, I feel like I'm wandering
around with part of me missing. It feels like
there's a cold chill in the air without you near,
the only warmth the days bring without you, is
the people I keep close. They give me blankets,
wrap me up in their love, and remind me I'm not
alone. But sometimes I feel most alone on days
with everyone around, like the chatter is too
much for my ears. I stand alone in a room full of
people and wish you were here, because you by
my side made the room full of light. The skies
are gray, the rooms are dimly lit, and I am just

waiting until I can crawl back into bed. Until
sleep washes over me because there I can be lost
in a sea with memories of you and me.

You'll find me

You'll find me at the last page of a book, because I'm too impatient to wait for good things.

You'll find me doing something stupid at high places while I forget I'm scared of heights.

You'll find me locked up in my room on weekends where my 16-year-old self left me.

You'll find me jumping at sudden noises and putting my fists up in response.

You'll find me staring at black coffee I won't drink but, buy it anyway because it reminds me of my dad.

You'll find me placing flowers on gravestones, with names who have long gone.

You'll find me adding wedding photos to a Pinterest board like I'm getting married tomorrow but in fact I'm just a hopeless romantic.

You'll find me curled up in a corner telling you
to go away, but in fact I actually want you to
stay.

You'll find me on a scale weighing myself, but
asking why I'm not enough.

You'll find me flipping through our photographs,
wondering why I always get second place.

You'll find me screaming my lungs out but all I
want is to be heard.

You'll find me saying I'm fine here alone, like
it's always been. But all I wanted was to be
loved.

we're both wrong and right

42

You're scared of commitment

I am scared of getting hurt

You're saying "I don't know"

While I'm holding a knife to your throat

And I don't know if we'll make it out of this.

I was never the same

I remember the night, I remember the day all our friends called me a liar.

I remember the days I cried alone, I remember you telling me it was my fault.

I remember the baby I no longer had and the light I lost.

I remember the night like it was yesterday

I could still replay it bit for bit in my mind

If my thoughts wanted to be cruel enough.

Someone sleeping in my bed still haunts me, a
lover breathing next to me is no longer
comforting

An arm wrapped around me is cold instead of
warm.

I jump at your touch as you tell me you love me.

Don't pretend to care for me after all you have
done, don't sit here and act like you did nothing,
that you didn't turn all our friends against me.

Don't sit acting like everything is fine, cause
even though you're gone, I'm still here.

Left bleeding with the thought in my mind of
you crawling on top of me like everything was
fine, like no was just a suggestion because I was
your girlfriend. So to you that meant you had all
the freedom you wanted with my body.

Ever since I was a little girl, men have always
treated me like I'm property.

But this,

I won't take any more, and I'm done with this
democracy on my body.

sunny days

On the days I'm thinking in the shower, talking a little louder, and wishing for sunny days. I'm thinking of you, and us, and we, and our, and every way I can group us together. Because together we can't be, and I'm here standing in the street, speaking your name to the moon, hoping the stars could match your light oh, how bright it shined. If I had one superpower, I think I'd stop time, to a place for just you and me. We could grow old there together, put the world on pause, and then maybe I wonder if we'd still stop. If we'd still drop, fall and break, if we'd even last the day. I wish we had lasted the year, but my tears, oh dear, a puddle with no rain. Such a shame to be crying on sunny days.

Movie memories

I wish I could record it
moments of you and me
Like my life was a movie like I could stop time.
I wish I could show you the parallels of the pain
you cause in my mind, how it looks just the
same every time.
If I could pop in a tape and hit rewind.
Maybe then you'd understand me this time.

Batting Cages

We're going back and forth, and then in the middle of it all, you remind me of him.

The bitter way he spoke to me, the harshness in his tone, the words spoken just to hurt me, it's all the same.

Looking at you like you're molding into him, I'm not sure whose face I'm looking at anymore.

I don't know why or how I've somehow picked the same person in different versions, I feel like I'm standing in a batting cage while you all take your place.

"First shot is free!" Like there's a sign on the wall.

But don't worry my frail heart will give you it all. Taking hit after hit until I fall.

Man-made Monster

I don't want to be the girl who screams at men
anymore, who fights too hard, and throws insults
like punches, that leave scars on your heart.

I do not wish to be her, who cries in rage, and
boils over disagreements.

I don't wish to be her, don't bring her back,
please call off the attack. You're pounding at my
door, forcing this war, please leave her, let her be
graceful. Her gentle hands were not made for
war, but a war she would win if need be.

Please, I don't need me to win, wrap me in your
arms instead, call off the attack with your words,
silence the voices in my head with your touch,
and tell them it's okay to put my weapons down.

Instead, he watches scared because he doesn't
know how to love her.

Her gentle hands turn into calloused bloody
weapons, and he realizes the fight is all she's
ever known.

I guess we're doomed in the end, but at least I
know I can hold my own.

Spoken lies

Tell me you love me please, wipe my tears.

Tell me you love me please, show me there is no fear.

Tell me you love me please, don't walk out that door.

Tell me you love me please, your kisses hurt me more.

Tell me you love me please, I can't take another broken promise.

Tell me you love me please, the ending is near.

Ball of yarn

My emotions get mixed up

I get a little twisted

My heart is like a ball of yarn

Holding it in my hands

And it still doesn't make sense

I try to untangle it but I only make it worse

I'm looking at all the strings

Wondering how it got this messy

I don't know how to fix it

Please help me

I'll take the help this time

If you'll let me

One conversation at a time

Your heart will mend mine.

Missing you, wondering what went wrong

Maybe I should have been softer
Maybe I should have been patient a little longer
Maybe I should have counted the petals on my
flowers a little slower

My Home

Home?

You wanna know what home looks like?

Home is the instant warmth of his skin

Home is brown eyes, that look hazelnut in the sunlight

Home is forest green

Home is sunsets and sunrise tangled in your scent

Home is comfortable and safe

Home is here with you

Was it worth it?

54

I will never be her

But I hope when you find the one to satisfy you

She'll still taste like me.

We Hurt Equally

Men get hurt too,

I've watched the men in my life fall apart

I've watched them tell hurtful stories and shed tears.

You're a monster to think they aren't people with feelings as well

I've held lovers in my arms while they fell apart

I've watched brothers hold in tears because they were told crying wasn't allowed

because they were told emotions were not allowed.

I hope you lose sleep over the gentle men you've broken, whom you told weren't allowed to be human.

Hazel

56

I hope you see my eyes in every shade of green,
I hope the sunset reminds you of me, I hope you
realize I was the best you ever had, and I hope it
kills you once you realize you'll never find a girl
like me.

Damaged goods

57

Do you love all the bad parts of me? All the scary things that keep me up at night, the things I feel trapped reliving in my head over and over again. I'm sorry you received the damaged parts of me, just know I'm trying to keep her at bay, but sometimes she knocks the door down, and I hope you'll love me a little more on those days. Because on those days I'll be fighting to close the door again, to lock her away in hopes she doesn't come another day.

Words unsaid

58

It's scary to think about wanting something so bad you'd die for it.

If I was promised that I'd be with you in the afterlife

I'd go in a heartbeat.

Haunted

59

I still look for you in everything

I still think of you in every place we went

You're like a ghost

You live here in my heart

I can't let you go

bury the love

people say you should never go back to your
exes, but they come around every once in a
while, asking for friendship, or asking to finally
bury our love. parts of me wish they never
would, that i would just block them out of my
life forever, but no one tells you how hard it is to
feel nothing, to only feel anger, or to only feel
pain for them. they each know another version
of me, for every change i've gone through, and
every pain i've felt in those versions, and for
some of my worse moments. it makes you want
to crawl back to that version of yourself that you
find comfort in, and to someone who can only
understand the old you and not the new. i'm
saying don't do it, don't go backwards, run away,
and never look back. your future is waiting for
you past the sunset.

Seeing ghosts

You shook, you trembled, you spoke her name in
your sleep.

I saw her in your eyes while you looked at me,

I noticed you looked in every empty space.

You looked lost, your face lit up, then dropped,
you realized it was me and not her.

I smiled through the pain you brought me

I hope you get your happy ending, but
it won't be with me.

I'd Tell her

If I could speak to the little girl who locked herself away, I'd tell her it was okay to stay.

That people don't show up, but it's okay.

Because there will be others who beg you to stay.

I'd tell her that he loved her, more than anything in the world and if he could he would've always chosen his little girl.

I'd tell her that sometimes life isn't fair, that life is bittersweet.

I'd tell her that being a hopeless romantic hurts your heart, but damn on the days it doesn't, it wonderfully tears you apart.

I'd tell her that anger has a second face, and that face is grief.

I'd tell her how there's a lot of days it absolutely shatters us, but I'd also tell her that life is bittersweet, that your heart is gonna hurt while healing, and it's gonna heal while not hurting.

Bottom of the well

Most days feel like I'm sitting at the bottom of
the well

waiting for someone to throw down a rope

scratch marks all over the walls trying to crawl
my way out

defeated at the bottom

curled up starved for love and for care

I haven't seen the light in days, nothing but the
dirty ground.

People walk past and tease me
throwing down drops of water, pieces of bread,
and inches of rope but not enough to get me out.

They laugh at my face, the hurt that never goes
away, the tear-stained cheeks that never stop
flowing, and
with every bit and piece that gets thrown, it's
just never enough, and my bitter heart sinks
down further,

until the screams that echo fill my mind, I am
stuck. I am here. I am a part of the well.

64

A Star-filled sky on the hill side

I'm ending our chapter

Going back to the place where it all started

And leaving your heart to the skies.

Child of the skies

On the days I feel most broken

The sky closes up

It feels my heart break

And sheds tears in my name.

Late night car rides

67

I wonder if you play that song and remember me

I wonder if you sing along and miss me dearly

I wonder if you still hear me singing and if it haunts you all night long.

Loving me for benefits

They like me because looking at my body brings
them pleasure

because the comfort I give feels like their
mothers

because the kindness I bring benefits them

because it's convenient

because my presence is intoxicating.

They do not like me for my eyes

for my smarts

for my laugh

for my heart

Or for my soul.

She is

69

She is soft smiles, rose petals, coffee in the
morning, sweaters on a cold night, she has fire in
her eyes, wonder in her heart, she'll build you
up, and burn you all at once.

Love was not what you gave

70

I should have known

Cause every time you spoke

I felt myself get smaller

And smaller

The way I changed my tone of voice

Stood up straight when you'd walk into the room

That wasn't love

It was control

It was fear

Tired of shutting out love

I think I'm tired of shutting out love, tired of being alone, and having nowhere to really call home

I no longer want to flinch at the touch of a hug from a friend, I no longer want to not accept fist bumps and compliments

I want forehead kisses, all the cuddles in the world, I want hugs and I miss you's

I want, "are we getting lunch this weekend together" without hesitation at all

I want "I'll pick you up at 8" when you call

I want to fill the rooms of my home with enough love for me, and enough love for everyone very dear to me

I don't want to regret it, I don't want to hold back, I wanna paint that picture, buy that gift, make that phone call, and never look back

Never look back and say "what if they leave"

That's okay, cause all of this light lit up their
way, and they'll always remember there's a room
in my home with their name.

Sunflowers

73

I don't look at sunflowers the same

I still remember the necklace you gave me

You treated me well, it's what I should have wanted

But I didn't

And I just carried too much baggage

You met me in a time I was falling apart

My world was falling apart and that was all I saw

Sorry for the crossfire

Mental illness

Sometimes on a daily basis I feel like I become a bitter reminder to people, that while I look like running through fields of flowers, painfully on the inside I am not. I'm death and destruction, I'm black matter, and horrible thoughts.

Missing you, always.

Sometimes on the days it gets bad, I get the urge to get on a plane, to sit at your grave, as if the weight of the silence would fill the void of wanting to run into your arms.

Dial tone

I told myself,

"do your own thing and don't wait for him"

But I still stayed up waiting for a text, for a call,
for a care.

I told myself,

"Don't give up anything for anyone, do what you
want to do in life"

But I still changed my plans the day you called,
cleared my schedule, and waited for
disappointment.

I told myself,

"Let him show you who he is, don't say
anything"

I still ripped my own heart out, shedding tears
on the floor, you showed me you didn't care, and
I still came crawling back for more.

Wishful thinking

That feeling when you're watching your favorite
heartbreak movie

Probably for the fifth time

And it's getting closer to the ending

You're hoping they get their happy ending,

But no matter how many times you've watched
it,

It stays the same,

And no matter how many times you wish it
would change it never will.

That's how love feels sometimes.

Refusal

I refuse to go back, to hiding in the bathroom with whatever sharp object I found that day, to crying out on the floor until I couldn't breathe, to locking the door of every room I went in. I'll never go back to curled up in a ball while they scream and pound on the door, to being told I'm a worthless excuse for a person, to being walked on and talked over. I'm not her anymore, I won't take your beatings anymore, I'll be the one standing with bloody knuckles.

Bedtime thoughts

79

I often think while lying in bed
Of just how many bodies have laid next to me
All who have brought me pain
Who have declared love
And left like they didn't love at all
I wish I could burn the mattress
Burn the sheets
Peel my flesh
And maybe
Just maybe
The feeling would go away
The pain would stop
The thought would leave

Trust issues

I'd ask if I fell

Would you catch me

But I never fall without my own safety net.

My heart is a black hole

81

Grab my throat

I'd stare you down

I'd still love you

Even as the light leaves my eyes

That's my fault

That's my pain

My heart is so big, I'd love you even as you killed me.

Not a princess

I am not the sweet princess

I am not frail

I am not small

I am a warrior

A knight in hiding

I face monsters you could not fathom

I am not easily broken

If you cannot walk this path with the tragedies I face

Then do not attempt to walk at all

Locked box

I'm easily scared, can't tell you I won't run away.

I'm superstitious, your change in tone, and your
anger are all I know.

Won't lay it all on the line, that's too much for
me to bear.

Keep a sword behind my back, just in case
you've come too close.

Always standing with my fists up, you'll never
see them down.

Won't let you get close enough to feel, never
close enough to swim in the ocean of my
emotions.

This might mean I am broken, a brokenness that
doesn't go away.

Maybe I'll fade with each day, better a friend
than a lover, cause friends don't really know
each other.

Holding them at arm's length

Standing at the doorway of my darkest parts

I won't let you in, I won't let you know.

This battle here, I shall always face alone.

Though there may be no end, I can't let you in.

Blood on my sword, tears in my eyes, I'd rather
hold this between us than beg for help.

Maybe that is my flaw, maybe that is my fault.

Maybe that is my brokenness unchanged.

Forever yours, for forever more, with deepest
regrets, I am sorry I'm not all you wanted and
more.

www.ingramcontent.com/pod-product-compliance
Lightning Source LLC
La Vergne TN
LVHW041223200726
843507LV00013B/2558